GLOBALIZATION AND THE NATURE OF WAR

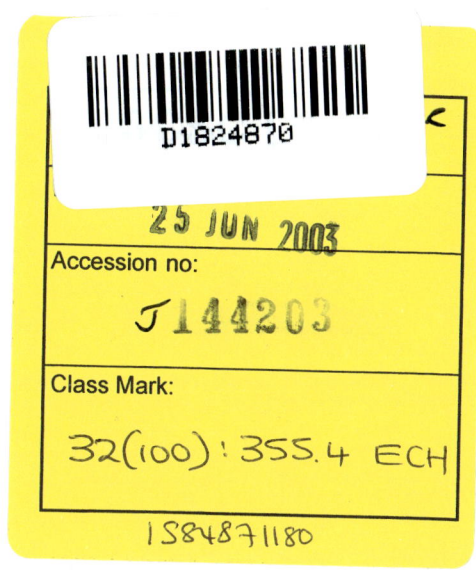

LTC Antulio J. Echevarria II

March 2003

*****

Comments pertaining to this report are invited and should be forwarded to: Director, Strategic Studies Institute, U.S. Army War College, 122 Forbes Ave., Carlisle, PA 17013-5244. Copies of this report may be obtained from the Publications Office by calling (717) 245-4133, FAX (717) 245-3820, or be e-mail at *Rita.Rummel@carlisle.army.mil*

*****

Most 1993, 1994, and all later Strategic Studies Institute (SSI) monographs are available on the SSI Homepage for electronic dissemination. SSI's Homepage address is: *http://www.carlisle.army. mil/ssi/index.html*

*****

The Strategic Studies Institute publishes a monthly e-mail newsletter to update the national security community on the research of our analysts, recent and forthcoming publications, and upcoming conferences sponsored by the Institute. Each newsletter also provides a strategic commentary by one of our research analysts. If you are interested in receiving this newsletter, please let us know by e-mail at *outreach@carlisle.army.mil* or by calling (717) 245-3133.

ISBN 1-58487-118-0

FOREWORD

Perhaps the single most important phenomenon of the 21st century is globalization. It is clearly redefining the international security environment, as well as many other aspects of human affairs. Yet, while analysts and scholars continue to study (and debate) its economic, social, and political effects, they have done comparatively little work concerning its impact on war, in particular the nature of war. In an effort to fill this gap, Lieutenant Colonel Antulio J. Echevarria II has written a monograph exploring the nature of war, and how it has changed as a result of globalization. He uses the Clausewitzian model of war's trinity (political guidance, chance, and enmity) as a framework for understanding the nature of war, a concept that has been only vaguely represented in defense literature. He then analyses the global war on terrorism via that framework. Lieutenant Colonel Echevarria concludes that the Clausewitzian trinity is alive and well. Globalization is strengthening the role that political guidance is playing in war, it may well increase the elements of chance and uncertainty, and it is clearly exacerbating basic feelings of enmity among different cultures. It is this last area that Lieutenant Colonel Echevarria sees as the most critical in the war on terrorism. If there is a center of gravity in this conflict, it is in the ideas that have fueled radical Islam.

The Strategic Studies Institute is pleased to publish this contribution to the debate on globalization's effect on war.

DOUGLAS C. LOVELACE, JR.
Director
Strategic Studies Institute

BIOGRAPHICAL SKETCH OF THE AUTHOR

ANTULIO J. ECHEVARRIA II, a lieutenant colonel in the U.S. Army, is currently assigned as the Director of Strategic Research at the Strategic Studies Institute. He graduated from the U.S. Military Academy in 1981, was commissioned as an armor officer, and has held a variety of command and staff assignments in Germany and Continental United States; he has also served as an assistant professor of European history at the U.S. Military Academy; Squadron S3 of 3/16 Cavalry; Chief of BN/TF and Bde Doctrine at the U.S. Army Armor Center at Fort Knox; as an action officer at the Army After Next project at HQ TRADOC, Ft. Monroe, VA; and as a speechwriter for the U.S. Army Chief of Staff. He is a graduate of the U.S. Army's Command and General Staff College, the U.S. Army War College, and holds M.A. and Ph.D. degrees in History from Princeton University. He has published articles in a number of scholarly and professional journals to include the *Journal of Strategic Studies*, *Journal of Military History*, *War in History*, *War & Society*, *Parameters*, *Joint Force Quarterly*, *Military Review*, and *Airpower Journal*. His book, *After Clausewitz: German Military Thinkers before the Great War*, was published by the University Press of Kansas in the spring of 2001.

SUMMARY

Just a few years into the new millennium, and it is already a truism to say that globalization—the spread of information and information technologies, along with greater public participation in economic and political processes—is transforming every aspect of human affairs. What is not yet clear, however, are the impacts of these trends, especially how they might affect the nature of war. Understanding the nature of war is important for more than academic reasons; the nature of a thing tends to define how it can and cannot be used, which, in the case of war, makes it extremely important to both political and military leaders. To answer the question of war's nature, one must turn to the famous Prussian philosopher of war, Carl von Clausewitz (1780-1831), who devoted more time than perhaps any other military theorist (contemporary or otherwise) to this topic.

The Clausewitzian Nature of War.  Subjective + objective

The most important aspect of Clausewitz's concept of war is that war has a dual nature, not in the bi-polar sense where wars can be limited or unlimited, but in the sense that derives from German philosophical traditions in which phenomena are considered to have objective and subjective natures. The objective nature of war includes those elements—such as violence, friction, chance, and uncertainty—that all wars have in common. Conflicts can range in kind from an all-out attack to a war of observation (peacekeeping), for instance, but each will have all of these elements present to one degree or another. By contrast, the subjective nature of war encompasses those elements— such as military forces, their doctrines, weapons, as well as the environments (land, sea, air, and danger) in which they fight—that make each war unique. Under Clausewitz's concept, the objective and subjective natures of war interact continuously. As a result, the nature of war cannot be separated from the means and the actors involved in its conduct.

In addition, war is shaped by three major forces (war's trinity) that also contribute to its nature: a subordinating or guiding influence (policy), the play of chance and probability, and enmity or basic hostility. Each is present in the current global war on terrorism.

The Element of Subordination—War as a Political Instrument.

Globalization has actually increased the role of politics, both in determining the purpose for and influencing the actual conduct of war. Both President George W. Bush and terrorist leader Osama bin Laden have released statements that link their actions to very explicit political agendas. Hence, the conflict remains thoroughly political at every level and, thus far at least, throughout every operational phase. Furthermore, this trend does not appear likely to reverse itself.

The Element of Hostility—Blind Natural Force.

The element of blind natural force is playing a decisive role in the global war on terrorism. Globalization has, among other things, contributed to the creation of fertile breeding grounds for terrorism as some groups try to resist its encroachment. Despite successful operations in Afghanistan and elsewhere, Al Qaeda's ideology remains intact and attractive to young Muslims. By comparison, the U.S. populace, which lacked any deep-seated feelings of hostility prior to September 11, 2001, is now being psychologically prepared (one can argue how well) by its political leadership for a long fight. The war against global terrorism is thus foremost a battle of ideas—ideas powerful enough to provoke violent emotions. Consequently, it is within this arena that the war will be won or lost.

The Elements of Chance and Uncertainty—Military Forces.

For the United States and its Western allies, the elements of chance and uncertainty manifest themselves through traditional, if transforming, military and law enforcement organizations. For non-state actors such as Al Qaeda, on the other hand, chance and uncertainty are personified in irregular forces buoyed by a broad, religion-based ideology, an extensive organizational and operational infrastructure, and a multinational membership. While information technologies provide more data to decisionmakers and their constituencies, without analysis and synthesis such data are inadequate. The total amount of information—which includes irrelevant and incorrect information—might increase by a certain percent, but knowledge grows by the same percent.

Conclusions.

Globalization is strengthening the role that politics will play in war by affording it the capability to exert greater real-time control over military operations. Globalization is also making the element of hostility more critical. Political leaders can now mobilize hostile passions more quickly and over a larger area than hitherto, particularly in areas "suffering" from the spread of globalization. Finally, contrary to expectation, the increase in information that globalization brings may well intensify the play of chance and probability in war.

Even with globalization, war remains essentially Clausewitzian in nature. It is still a dynamic expression of political wills in conflict. The challenge is to defeat volatile, extremist ideas. Hence, the center of gravity in the global war on terrorism is ideological in nature. The United States and its strategic partners must take the fight to the enemy on that front and win there decisively.

GLOBALIZATION AND THE NATURE OF WAR

Just a few years into the new millennium and it is already a truism to say that globalization—the spread of information and information technologies, along with greater public participation in economic and political processes—is transforming every aspect of human affairs.[1] Indeed, globalization is enhancing the real and virtual mobility of people, things, and ideas and is increasing social, political, and economic interconnectedness worldwide. From 1980 to 1996, for example, the percentage of the world's population that travels internationally on a regular basis rose from 6.5 percent to 10 percent.[2] Similarly, the number of personal computers connected to the internet has been growing at a rate of nearly 70 percent per year for more than 30 years.[3] The associated spread of democratic ideas and free market values helped increase the total number of democracies in the world by 14 percent within the last decade alone.[4] Furthermore, considerable evidence suggests that globalization is making national and regional economies more interdependent, thereby giving rise to an integrated world market economy.[5] Clearly, then, globalization is changing how we interact with our world.

What is not yet clear, however, are the impacts of these trends. While the world may indeed have more democracies than ever before, how many of them have stable regimes with established civil societies where strong traditions exist conforming to the rule of law? As the example of Weimar Germany shows, newly formed democracies can rapidly reverse course and transform into dangerous autocratic regimes. While there is some validity to the view that "established democracies do not go to war with other democracies," the number of established democracies is relatively small.[6] Also, while globalization has improved general wealth, raised living standards, and increased life expectancy across the world, 60 percent of the world's wealth continues to travel back and forth among the developed countries, giving them the greater share of benefits. The poor may be richer, but the rich are richer still; and the gap between them is growing.[7] What is more, as the First and Second World Wars demonstrate, economic interconnectedness and continuous growth do not necessarily preclude conflict.

Despite its apparent positive impact on the spread of democracy and free-market economies, globalization might produce a more dangerous and unpredictable world, especially if the cultural backlash it has generated thus far gathers more momentum. This world might be characterized by shifting power relationships, *ad hoc* security arrangements, and an ever-widening gap between the richest and poorest nations.[8] A number of new democracies—lacking strong traditions for maintaining checks and balances—might, for example, collapse after only transitory successes. Transnational threats, such as international crime syndicates, terrorist networks, and drug cartels, could continue to grow in strength and influence, thriving among autocratic, weak, or so-called failed states. And, ethnic rivalries, nationalism, religious-based antagonisms, and competition for scarce resources, including water, could go unresolved. Thus, serious crises would undoubtedly arise, especially as the world's population continues to grow.

On the other hand, globalization could give rise to a more stable world in which national interests merge into the general aim of promoting peace, stability, and economic prosperity.[9] In this world, the rule of law and the existence of pluralistic political systems would continue to spread; and the number of free-market economies would expand, distributing economic prosperity still further. Even if this "Utopia" should materialize, a number of crises—some of which will undoubtedly require military intervention—will most likely have had to occur beforehand, since most autocratic regimes will probably not surrender power without a fight. Moreover, as the 1999 Kosovo crisis

2

demonstrated, even relatively small states armed primarily with conventional weapons can pose significant security challenges to a superpower and its strategic partners.[10] The world need not devolve into a "clash of civilizations" or a "coming anarchy," therefore, in order for military power to continue to play a significant role in the future.[11]

In any case, globalization will surely continue and may even accelerate if data concerning the rate of technological change are any indication.[12] As numerous studies and strategic papers have pointed out, globalization is already changing how wars are being fought in the 21st century, making them more dangerous than in any previous era.[13] At a minimum, the greater mobility of people, things, and ideas will mean increased mobility for nonstate actors, weapons of mass destruction, and radical fundamentalism of all types.

In fact, the U.S. Department of State currently reports that more than 60 active terrorist groups exist (with some 100,000 members); and over one-third of them have the capacity for global reach.[14] Furthermore, today's terrorists have proven very adaptive, learning from previous generations, and changing their tactics in response to new anti-terrorist measures.[15] Globalization clearly offers them some extraordinary capabilities to communicate and coordinate their efforts.

Globalization also facilitates the proliferation of destabilizing capabilities, such as weapons of mass destruction or mass effect. Eleven countries currently have nuclear weapons programs; thirteen more are actively seeking them.[16] More than 25 countries now possess ballistic missiles, and over 75,000 cruise missiles are in existence, with the number expected to rise to between 80,000 and 90,000 by 2010.[17] Also, at least 17 countries—including the so-called "Axis of Evil"—currently have active chemical and biological weapons programs, and the number is rising.[18] As the Assistant Secretary of State for Non-proliferation recently explained, despite the provisions

3

of the Nuclear Non-proliferation Treaty and the Chemical and Biological Weapons conventions, proliferation of chemical, biological, radiological, nuclear and high explosive/high yield weapons continues worldwide: "There is an intense sort of cooperation that goes on among countries that are trying to acquire such weapons."[19] For example, China and North Korea have long contributed to the proliferation of chemical and biological weapons, both for strategic leverage against the United States and for economic advantages.[20] Thus, globalization assists some powerful motives that run counter to nonproliferation efforts.

Biological weapons, especially, pose a serious threat not only to human populations, but also to agriculture and livestock. Unfortunately, U.S. crops lack genetic diversity, rendering them vulnerable to disease. Furthermore, the nation's centralized feeding and marketing practices make livestock extremely vulnerable to a biological attack. If such an attack were to occur, a devastating ripple effect would surely spread throughout the global economy since the United States produces 30-50 percent of the world's foodstuffs.[21]

Globalization has also introduced a new form of warfare: cyber-war. More than 30 countries—including Russia, China, and several so-called rogue states—have developed or are developing the capability to launch strategic-level cyber attacks.[22] The interconnectedness of many nations' infrastructures means that a successful cyber attack against a single sector in one country could result in adverse effects in other sectors within the same country, or those of its neighbors. Indeed, intended (and unintended) adverse effects could well travel globally.[23]

If globalization is making war more dangerous and adding new dimensions to it (such as cyber space), is it in some way changing the *nature* of war? What exactly *is* the nature of war? These questions are of more than a purely academic interest, since the nature of a thing tends to define how it can and cannot be used.

To answer the question of war's nature, we must turn to the famous Prussian philosopher of war, Carl von Clausewitz (1780-1831), who devoted more time than perhaps any other military theorist (contemporary or otherwise) to understanding the nature of war. Western theories of the nature of war seem to derive—in one way or another—from Clausewitz's own work on the subject. Despite its length and its sometimes ponderous prose, his masterwork, *Vom Kriege* (*On War*), has been cited by the majority of contemporary scholars and defense analysts. In fact, his most popular observation that "war is the mere continuation of policy by other means" now forms the core of the western, and in particular the American, view of war.[24] This belief is reflected in the bulk of the modern literature on war, including the memoirs of prominent military commanders.[25] The dominant—and in many ways tacit—understanding of this passage is that war is foremost a political act and that policy alone determines (or ought to determine) the object for which a war is to be fought, the scale of effort to be exerted, and the means to be employed. Since policy gives war purpose and direction, so the reasoning goes, it forms the *central* element in war's nature.

This belief is largely a post-Vietnam phenomenon, however. Prior to that, most military writers considered war's nature as something akin to Clausewitz's concept of absolute war, an idealized extreme, but one that some claim was nearly realized in the total wars of the 20th century.[26] A popular view emerged within the U.S. military that the nature of war—nasty and brutal—was essentially unchanging.[27] Only its character—the way it is waged—transformed over time. A corollary of this view was that low-intensity and guerrilla conflicts were not "valid" types of wars and so professional militaries should avoid them; true war demanded full mobilization of the popular will and a strategy of going "all-out" against one's opponent, even in conflicts involving so-called limited aims.[28] The post-

Vietnam renaissance of Clausewitz in military and scholarly literature surely contributed to the general awareness of the centrality of politics in his theory of war.[29]

Yet, some critics of Clausewitz—such as historian John Keegan—have maintained that, for many societies, war serves more of a religious or cultural function than a political one.[30] Keegan rejects Clausewitz's idea that war is an extension of politics, claiming that it is "incomplete, parochial and ultimately misleading."[31] According to Keegan, politics in many cases serves culture, which he defines very broadly as the "shared beliefs, values, associations, myths, taboos, imperatives, customs, traditions, manners and ways of thought, speech and artistic expression which ballast every society."[32] Defined this broadly, culture would be responsible for much, indeed. He maintains that some societies make war simply because it is an integral part of their culture to do so; thus wars take the character and shape that cultures cause them to take. Accordingly, war itself has no specific nature.[33]

Other critics, such as historians Martin van Creveld and Russell Weigley, have taken direct issue with the concept of politics. Van Creveld attempts to paint Clausewitz into a corner. He argues that Clausewitz's dictum about war serving politics can mean only that war is the *rational* extension of the will of the *state*; otherwise, the dictum is nothing more than a meaningless cliché. Accordingly, if Clausewitz's dictum only pertains to the rational will of the state, it fails to account for the wealth of irrational motives that drive war. In short, according to van Creveld, Clausewitz is only describing what the nature of war should be, not what it actually is. Therefore, his theory has no practical value.[34] Unfortunately, as we shall see, van Creveld, like so many others, has misinterpreted *On War*.

For his part, Weigley maintains that politics tends to become an instrument of war rather than the other way around. In an essay assessing military effectiveness in the First and Second World Wars—genuine global conflicts

6

within the 20th-century context—Weigley concluded that "War once begun has always tended to generate a politics of its own: to create its own momentum, to render obsolete the political purposes for which it was undertaken, and to erect its own political purposes."[35] According to this view, then, military necessity and the dynamics of conflict, particularly conflict on a global scale or for unlimited aims, tend to constrain and subordinate policy. Yet, Weigley's assessment ultimately amounts to less a valid criticism of Clausewitz's idea than an unconscious affirmation of it, for, as the Prussian theorist explained, in the course of a war, political aims are apt to change, at times even radically. This alteration would be more apparent than real, however, since it would merely reflect the fact that political and military aims had coincided. In other words, policy itself is not subordinated as much as, locked in a life-or-death struggle, it assumes a "war-like" character. Hence, under Clausewitz's concept, policy, which is also of two characters— one aggressive and one placatory—is just as present in wars of unlimited aims as it is in wars of limited ones.[36]

The Clausewitzian Nature of War.

A re-examination of Clausewitz's ideas about the nature of war helps dispel these misunderstandings; it also uncovers a surprisingly durable and versatile concept, one that remains valid for the 21st century. Inexplicably, the most important aspect of Clausewitz's nature of war has gone unnoticed—that war has a dual nature, not in the bi-polar sense where wars can be limited or unlimited, but in the sense that derives from German philosophical traditions in which phenomena are considered to have objective and subjective natures.[37] The former pertains to those aspects of a phenomenon that are universally valid; the latter concerns those that are true only for a specific time and space. The objective nature of war thus includes those elements—such as violence, friction, chance, and uncertainty—that all wars have in common, no matter where or when they are fought. Conflicts can range in kind from an all-out attack to a war of observation (peace-keeping), for instance, but each will have all of these elements present to one degree or another.

By contrast, the subjective nature of war encompasses those elements—such as military forces, their doctrines, weapons, as well as the environments (land, sea, air, and danger) in which they fight—that make each war unique. One way to grasp this construct is to think of objective elements as internal and subjective ones as external. Maritime conflicts, for instance, appear different externally from wars on land, but are nonetheless similar with respect to their internal characteristics. Even the same conflict can change its appearance over time as different combatants enter or leave the fight, or introduce new weapons, tactics, and techniques into the fray, as in the Thirty Years' War.

Interestingly, under Clausewitz's concept, the objective and subjective natures of war are closely connected to one another and interact continuously. New weapons or methods, for example, can increase or diminish the degree of violence or uncertainty, though probably never eliminate them entirely. Similarly, a war's political motives can cause the combatants to use, or refrain from using, certain types of weapons or tactics, as in the Cold War where both the United States and the Soviet Union essentially established a number of treaties designed to prevent escalation to nuclear war. Thus, the interaction between the objective and subjective natures of war is a dynamic one. In Clausewitz's words, war's subjective and objective natures make it "more than a simple chameleon" that only changes its nature partially.[38] A chameleon might change its color, for instance, but its internal organs would remain the same. War's internal tendencies, on the other hand, can change in intensity, proportion, and relative role as the external features themselves transform. Therefore, under Clausewitz's system, the nature of war cannot be separated from the means and the actors involved in its conduct.

The Clausewitzian Trinity.

Since wars do not occur in a vacuum but in the complexities of the physical world, Clausewitz devoted comparatively little time to examining war—along with its nature—as an isolated activity. Instead, he discussed the nature of war via another well-known concept—the "wondrous" or "remarkable" trinity (*wunderliche Dreifaltigkeit*)—which he also considered as a foundation for a theory of war. The trinity is built on the same objective-subjective construct discussed above, which may make it difficult to understand at first blush.[39] In the objective sense, the trinity consists of three dynamic forces: a subordinating or guiding influence; the play of chance and probability; and the force of basic hostility. As Clausewitz explained:

> War is thus not only a genuine chameleon, since it alters its nature somewhat in each particular case, it is also, in its overall manifestations, a wondrous trinity with regard to its predominant tendencies, which consist of the original violence of war's nature, namely, hatred and hostility, which can be viewed as a blind natural force; of the play of probabilities and of chance, which make it into an unpredictable activity; and of the subordinating nature of a political instrument whenever it submits to pure reason.[40]

These forces come into play in every war, though the role of one is sometimes more pronounced or influential than the others. By introducing the trinity, Clausewitz moves from discussing war as a thing-in-itself (in isolation), an approach that was well within the German philosophical tradition, to concluding that war cannot be properly understood as a thing-in-itself. The trinity thus tells us that war's nature is inseparable from the historical and socio-political contexts in which it arises, and that no tendency is *a priori* more influential than any other. Thus, to single out policy or politics as the central element of war's nature is simply not Clausewitzian.

Viewed from a subjective standpoint, these tendencies manifest themselves in three ways: through the government (*die Regierung*), which attempts to direct war toward some objective; through military actors, such as the commander (*der Feldherr*) and his army (*sein Heer*), who must deal with the unpredictability of combat; and through the populace (*das Volk*), who act as a reservoir of the emotional power necessary to sustain a serious struggle. However, these elements assume variable forms over time and among different cultures.[41] Also, the term "government," as Clausewitz used it, stands for any ruling body, any "agglomeration of loosely associated forces," or any "personified intelligence."[42] Similarly, the military represents not only the trained, semi-professional armies of the Napoleonic era, but any warring body in any era. Likewise, Clausewitz's references to the "populace" pertain to the populations of any society or culture in any period of history.

The phrase "war is the mere continuation of policy by other means" requires further elucidation because it, more than any other, has come to represent the essence of Clausewitz's thought. In the German language, the word *Politik* can mean both *policy* and *politics*. While we might instantly recognize the difference between the two—the first is a product, the other a process—that distinction does not always appear in English translations. In Clausewitz's usage, the term *Politik* also has objective and subjective aspects.[43] In the objective sense, *Politik* means the extension of the will of the ruler through a process—both formal and informal—of arriving at a decision to pursue a goal. In the subjective sense, *Politik* clearly means a specific policy, an actual manifestation of politics that can vary from era to era and from people to people based on the influence of culture, ideology, geography, tradition, personality, and skill, among others. Thus, for Clausewitz, *Politik* encompasses more than mere policy, or a rational calculation of ends, ways, and means. In fact, he considered it "an art" in which human "judgment"— influenced by internal "qualities of mind and character"—comes into play.[44] It was also influenced by external factors such as the "characteristics" of a governing body's geo-political position as well as the general mind-set of the "spirit of the age."[45]

Clausewitz went on to explain that *Politik* was at work in Napoleon Bonaparte's imperialistic wars of expansion, just as well as in the raids of tribal plunder and conquest waged by the semi-nomadic Tartars.[46] While the policy aims of the Tartar tribes might have been less sophisticated than those of Bonaparte, they nonetheless derived from similar factors. Tartar warfare, for instance, reflected available resources (means), the tribes' geopolitical position as a composite of Turkish and Mongol peoples in Central Asia, their nomadic culture and traditions, and the religious influence of Islam.[47] Clausewitz's use of *Politik* thus represents the collective strengths and weaknesses of a body of people, to include its resources, alliances and treaties, and its own decisionmaking processes, as well as the skill and personalities of its policymakers. In a sense, *Politik* was for Clausewitz what culture (defined above) is for Keegan.

The Clausewitzian Nature of War and Globalization.

Clausewitz thus arrived at his concept of war's nature by first assuming that it did indeed have one. His analyses of historical conflicts validated that assumption by revealing that each war had characteristics in common with all others, though those characteristics might vary in terms of their relative dominance and intensity. Because the Clausewitzian nature of war has internal and external elements that are at once variable and able to influence one another, it captures the dynamism of real war as much as any theoretical concept can. Accordingly, it is more suitable for understanding the nature of war in today's global environment than any of the alternatives mentioned earlier.

The Element of Subordination—War as a Political Instrument.

The war against Al Qaeda and other terrorist groups of global reach represents the first conflict of the 21st century in which the characteristics of globalization—the enhanced mobility of people, things, and ideas—have come into play. It is certainly a war that neither side can afford to lose. The political objectives of the combatants reflect that realization, even if neither side has fully mobilized all of its forces to date. Sources indicate that, even though it is not necessarily bent on the immediate total destruction of the United States, Al Qaeda will never compromise and will continue to fight until all religious apostasy is eliminated, all illegitimate or corrupt Islamic regimes are replaced by a unified Muslim polity and Caliphate, and all infidels are driven from Muslim holy lands. [48] The United States is seen as a major source of support for apostatic regimes and, hence, weakening it politically and economically is essential for success. In order to ensure ultimate success, however, it might be necessary to have a final showdown with the "great Satan." For its part, the United States will not accept anything less than the complete neutralization, if not destruction, of Al Qaeda. Contrary to what historians such as Martin van Creveld have argued, therefore, the proliferation of weapons of mass destruction and the emergence of powerful nonstate actors, such as Al Qaeda, do not mean the end of decisive warfare or of major wars among states.[49] Instead, we find a general shift toward less overt and more protracted forms of conflict, while, at the same time, major powers such as the United States emphasize a greater willingness to take unilateral preemptive action or to respond to attacks involving weapons of mass destruction in any manner deemed appropriate, to include massive retaliation against major states.[50]

Moreover, instead of culture displacing politics as the primary force behind conflict, globalization has actually increased the latter's role, both in determining the purpose for and influencing the actual conduct of war. Both President George W. Bush and terrorist leader Osama bin Laden have released statements that link their actions to very explicit political agendas. Both are clearly using war to achieve political ends, rather than to satisfy a cultural impulse to wage war, as Keegan argues. To be sure, culture and politics are inextricably linked in this conflict. Al Qaeda's leadership might have sought to provoke a massive U.S. military response to the attacks of September 11, which it could then portray as an assault on Islam. This general assault, it was hoped, would inspire the entire Islamic world to rise up against the West.[51] Indeed, the West, conscious of this possibility, has taken great pains to portray the conflict as a war against terror tactics rather than a war against Islam. And, it must continue to do so. Otherwise, the conflict between Al Qaeda and the West may indeed escalate into a more dangerous "clash of civilizations." Nonetheless, the fact remains that both sides are using war as a political instrument, that is, they are subordinating its conduct to the achievement of political ends.

Political leaders on both sides can also have real-time access to military actions as they unfold, though one would hope that in the case of Al Qaeda the access would be less secure.[52] Still, both sides can more or less communicate their intentions to their operatives in the field and thus influence the course of events throughout every phase of a military operation, no matter where it occurs. This capability means that political direction of a campaign *can* span time and distance to influence the smallest of details, not that it *should*. Moreover, the public statements by President Bush and bin Laden's periodic releases of video messages through Al Jazeera demonstrate that each can address his support base to give it guidance or motivation, or to garner further support, while at the same time challenging or vexing his opponents. Hence, the conflict remains thoroughly political at every level and, thus far at least, throughout every operational phase. Furthermore, this trend does not appear likely to reverse itself.

The Element of Hostility—Blind Natural Force.

In the global war on terrorism, the element of blind natural force is playing the decisive role. Globalization has, among other things, contributed to the creation of fertile breeding grounds for terrorism as some groups try to resist its encroachment. Al Qaeda has associated the United States with the spread of globalization, which it sees as a form of decadence. Building on the perception that Islamic society's current political and economic problems are the result of the West's decadent values and duplicitous policies, Al Qaeda has penetrated Islamic nongovernmental organizations and woven itself into the social, political, and religious fabric of Muslim societies. Consequently, it has managed to create a substantial support base that may enable it to regenerate itself indefinitely.[53] Despite the arrest of hundreds of operatives in North America and abroad since the attacks of September 11, 2001, for example, Al Qaeda has created new cells and reconstituted older ones.[54] While operations in Afghanistan and elsewhere have led to the killing or capture of some 16 of its 25 key leaders, Al Qaeda's ideology remains intact and will probably continue to draw young Muslims.[55]

Evidence also suggests that Muslim extremism, or Islamism as some authorities identify it, has been moving from the margins of the Islamic political spectrum toward the center, so that bin Laden and other key terrorist leaders may enjoy considerable empathy, if not sympathy, regarding their words and actions.[56] The Islamist's mindset is that the current war is one in which God's warriors—the *mujahidin*—are heroically fighting the forces of Satan: U.S. troops.[57] In this war, civilian populations of both sides are more than a manifestation or a reservoir of "blind natural force." They have become the primary target in both a physical and a psychological sense for Al Qaeda and a

14

psychological sense for the United States. With what has been described as a "virus-like ability to infect indigenous groups," Al Qaeda has turned itself into an ideological weapon that evidently excels in the generation of propaganda to support its cause.[58] By comparison, the U.S. populace, which lacked any deep-seated feelings of hostility prior to September 11, 2001, is now being psychologically prepared (one can argue how well) by its political leadership for a long fight in which conditions might get worse—particularly if an attack on Iraq or other "rogue" states occurs—before they get better. Indeed, some of the current political rhetoric of the administration and its supporters likens the war against terrorism to "World War IV."[59] In other words, the war against global terrorism is foremost a battle of ideas—ideas powerful enough to provoke violent emotions. Consequently, it is within this arena that the war will be won or lost.

The Elements of Chance and Uncertainty—Military Forces.

For the United States and its Western allies, the elements of chance and uncertainty now manifest themselves through traditional, if transforming, military and law enforcement organizations. For nonstate actors such as Al Qaeda, on the other hand, chance and uncertainty are personified in irregular forces buoyed by a broad, religion-based ideology, an extensive organizational and operational infrastructure, and a multinational membership. Paradoxically, globalization and the spread of information technology have made it likely that both sides will generate more—rather than less—chance and uncertainty. Despite the existence of a vast technology-based intelligence and surveillance network, for example, a great deal of uncertainty still surrounds a single bit of tactical information of strategic importance, namely, the location of Osama bin Laden. Of course, the key to fighting a successful war on terrorism is intelligence, especially human intelligence. Unfortunately, for budgetary and cultural reasons, the United States scaled back its human intelligence efforts considerably some years ago.[60]

To be sure, information technologies now deliver more information than ever before to decisionmakers and their constituencies. Still, without analysis and synthesis, the information they provide is always inadequate. As Al Qaeda's attacks to date have shown, small terrorist cells can execute well-coordinated—and genuinely devastating— surprise assaults despite a vast intelligence network and the proliferation of information technologies.[61] Thus, we simply cannot make a direct, linear correlation between information and knowledge. The total amount of information—which includes irrelevant and incorrect information—may well increase by a certain percent, but that does not mean that knowledge grows by the same percent. It is often impossible to discern the quality or correctness of information until after the fact—when it can be compared to the way events actually unfolded.

We would do better to develop experienced judgment and learn to become comfortable with uncertainty—with things that we cannot know beyond a reasonable doubt—than to delude ourselves that our technology will deliver all the knowledge we need to achieve victory. Yet, experienced judgment takes time to develop; and we may not have that luxury in an era in which change seems to be occurring at an accelerating rate.[62] In other words, knowledge is not solely a function of available information. Merely throwing more information at the problem will not solve it. Contrary to what pundits have predicted, therefore, globalization and the spread of information technologies still have not eliminated the elements of chance and uncertainty in war. In some cases, in fact, these elements may increase, especially if opponents use misinformation more frequently as a counter to knowledge-based warfare.

Defense officials have repeatedly asserted that, on matters of combat, new thinking has yet to replace old. However, one should not act too hastily here. While many of today's weapons differ significantly from those of a century ago, several of the tactical and operational principles that underpin military doctrine still remain valid. Studies of the recent fighting in Afghanistan, for example, show that the principles of fire and movement that enabled soldiers to cross the deadly zone during the First World War have proven just as essential against entrenched Taliban and Al Qaeda forces.[63]

Nonetheless, at least one fundamental concept of Western military doctrine—Clausewitz's center of gravity—has some serious limitations and may have outlived its usefulness. For decades, the U.S. military in particular has wrongly defined the center of gravity as "a source of strength." Yet, Clausewitz's original notion of the center of gravity was more akin to that of a focal point, a place where energies come together to be redirected and refocused elsewhere.[64] It was neither a strength nor a weakness, per se, but it could be strong—well-protected—or not. Even with a redefinition, however, the concept may have only limited applicability in a globalized operational environment where opponents can fight in vast, distributed networks without necessarily being linked to one central authority, or to one another. Clausewitz's center of gravity concept depends on the condition that the enemy is connected enough to act as a single entity. By implication, when this was not the case, the concept did not apply.

Unfortunately, a globalized operational environment presents fewer cases in which enemies function as a single entity. Al Qaeda's global terrorist network adheres to the cellular, or cluster, model in which many cells exist, but the members of any particular cell do not necessarily know one another, or those in other cells. If one member is caught, the other members and other cells are not in danger.[65] Destroying Al Qaeda cells in Europe, therefore, will not necessarily cause those in Indonesia to collapse. In fact, destroying such distributed enemies in one location could lead to some extremely undesirable consequences, if those at other locations retaliate by discharging a weapon of mass destruction in a major city. Hence, the United States must think more globally—finding ways to hit as many enemy cells as simultaneously as possible. Furthermore, Al Qaeda's center of gravity might lie at its ideological core— its hatred of apostasy and its vision of a pan-Islamic empire—since that is what enables it to draw recruits and to support them. Yet, ideology is a difficult target to hit militarily. Still, if employed in combination with other elements of national power, military might can prove invaluable, even in this type of conflict. Military thinking has changed a great deal over the last decade. However, it has yet to relinquish certain linear concepts that no longer apply and to internalize the idea of fighting in a discontinuous, highly volatile environment. And, it must find better ways to combine the effects of military operations with those of economic, political, and informational actions as well.

Military thinking is not alone in this regard. The strategy of "ring vaccination" that officials in the Centers for Disease Control want to employ as a way to counter bio-attacks of smallpox and similar contagious diseases is an example of a similarly inappropriate linear concept.[66] In brief, the strategy calls for vaccinating only those individuals (such as emergency and medical personnel) who are or would likely come in contact with an infected person, thereby creating, in theory at least, a ring that will isolate the disease even before it is discovered. However, while this strategy proved effective in containing and eliminating natural outbreaks of smallpox in Asia and elsewhere, it will hardly work against an attack delivered simultaneously at multiple locations—at three or four major airports, sports arenas, or major shopping malls, for example. In a globalized world, as infected individuals travel about the country, the disease would spread too quickly for such containment measures to work.[67]

Accordingly, officials responsible for developing strategies for combating diseases, just as much as those for defeating highly decentralized enemies, must approach the problem from a global and nonlinear perspective.[68] One approach, of course, is a strategy of mass vaccination. At present, however, the smallpox vaccine is not without risk to certain populations, thereby making mass vaccination an unpopular solution. Clearly, a safer vaccine is needed, and quickly, not only for smallpox but for other contagious diseases. And, different strategies for defending against bio-attacks must be developed concurrently and war-gamed. When (if ever), for example, should the United States close its borders and cease all traffic in the event of a serious bio-attack? And for how long? What if a neighboring country is hit? How will the global economy be affected? These and similar questions must be considered in advance and factored into the development of any viable strategy.

All of this raises some questions about another key concept of Clausewitz, his views about the relative strengths of attack and defense. Clausewitz maintained that the defense was the stronger form of war because its advantages—cover and concealment, shorter lines of supply, time, preparation of the terrain—compensate for the defender's psychological and physical weaknesses, at least partially. Moreover, the defender's aim is self-preservation, an objective that he can achieve by merely persuading the attacker to abandon the fight. Self-preservation is a condition that exists before hostilities commence and, in some cases, remains intact even if the defender's military is defeated. The attacker, on the other hand, enjoys the advantages of initiative and surprise, but these are weighed down by the burden of attempting to subdue his opponent, a task more difficult than merely surviving, once hostilities commence.[69] Hence, while Clausewitz considered the defense stronger, he did not maintain that it was better. Defense is not necessarily decisive, for example, since an attacker, once persuaded to give up the fight, could renew his assaults at a later time.

Do Clausewitz's arguments still hold when the attacker is willing to pay more in blood than the defender and when he can operate in a highly mobile, global environment? As the preceding discussion has shown, globalization has rendered societies more vulnerable to attack. It is exceedingly expensive—perhaps impossibly so—to defend against every conceivable form of attack. Accordingly, a determined opponent now has more opportunities to seize the initiative and to achieve surprise, particularly if he is a relatively invisible nonstate actor. Moreover, if his aims fall short of all-out conquest and subjugation, as seems to be the case with Al Qaeda, he is free of the burdens traditionally associated with the attacker.

Nonetheless, Clausewitz was not wrong in his day, nor is he altogether wrong in the present. As he pointed out, attack and defense are not exclusive concepts: an offensive has aspects of defense; and a defensive involves elements of attack. A well-conducted defense, he wrote, usually consists of many offensive blows, such as counterattacks and spoiling attacks.[70] Similarly, the U.S. military, in conjunction with the Department of Homeland Security and other agencies, should develop an "active global defense-in-depth" concept, based on the principle that the best defense includes major elements of an aggressive offense. To succeed in the emerging global environment, a defensive strategy must tag and relentlessly track terrorists and their accomplices, keeping them on the run and denying them opportunities to plan, organize, and execute a major attack. Such a strategy must also include provisions for actively targeting the sources from which the terrorists' financing and other resources—such as personnel—come. And it must involve building cooperative security arrangements, both at home and abroad, that provide interlocking, even redundant, security measures over all critical areas. In other words, while globalization clearly favors the attack, one can find ways to make it assist the defense. Anything less may only offer the terrorists another opportunity to increase their learning curve.

Conclusions.

If the war on terrorism is any guide, globalization is changing the nature of war in several ways. First, it is strengthening the role that politics will play in war by affording it the capability to exert greater real-time control over military operations. Of course, this control will vary depending on the personalities involved as well as a combatant's ability to interdict its opponent's communications. Second, globalization is increasing the criticality of the element of hostility. Political leaders can now mobilize hostile passions more quickly and over a larger area than hitherto, particularly in areas "suffering" from the spread of globalization. Images and the ideas they convey may now be more decisive than the sword. Yet, it may prove more difficult to cool such passions than it did to ignite them. Finally, globalization means that opponents (even if they are neighbors) can now fight each other across global distances, in new dimensions, and with a broader array of weapons. These changes may amount to a net increase in the dual element of chance and uncertainty at all levels of war. It remains to be seen whether information technology will reduce or exacerbate this expansion. Certainly, skillful commanders and well-trained militaries still matter.

Yet, as has been shown, even with the rapidly spreading and intensifying effects of globalization, war remains essentially Clausewitzian in nature. It is still a dynamic expression of political wills in conflict, colliding via the means of organized violence with multinational populations serving both as resources and as targets. The forces of Islamic terrorism are fueled by volatile extremist ideas and, hence, the global war on terrorism remains at heart a conflict of opposing ideas. The United States and its strategic partners must take the fight to the enemy on that front and win there decisively.

ENDNOTES

1. Thomas Friedman, *The Lexus and the Olive Tree*, New York: Anchor, 2000, p. 9, offers a similar definition of globalization—as the dispersion and democratization of technology, information, and finance. See also Stephen J. Flanagan, Ellen L. Frost, and Richard L. Kugler, *Challenges of the Global Century: Report of the Project on Globalization and National Security*, Washington, DC: Institute for National Strategic Studies, 2001.

2. From 287 million in 1980 to 595 million in 1996; the world's population increased from 4.4 to 5.7 billion, or 30 percent, during the same period. James H. Mittelman, *The Globalization Syndrome: Transformation and Resistance*, Princeton: Princeton University Press, 2000, p. 21.

3. Robert Hobbes, "Hobbes' Internet Timeline," August 23, 2001, *http://www.zakon.org*, accessed February 21, 2003.

4. *A National Security Strategy for a Global Age*, The White House, December 2000, p. 2, claims that more than half of the world's population now lives under democratic rule. How much of the increase is due to globalization is open to debate.

5. Bruce R. Scott, "Measuring Globalization," *Foreign Policy*, Jan/Feb 2001, p. 56-65, points out the difficulty of measuring globalization. See also "Toward a Better Understanding of Globalization and the Third World," in *Global Transformation and the Third World*, Robert O. Slater, Barry M. Schutz, and Steven R. Dorr, eds., Boulder: Lynne Reinner, 1993, pp. 5-7.

6. The view that democracies do not go to war with each other is defended in Donald M. Snow, *World Politics in a New Century: The Shape of the Future*, 3rd Ed., New York: M.E. Sharpe, 1999, p. 34. Bruce R. Scott, "The Great Divide in the Global Village," *Foreign Affairs*, Vol. 80, No. 1, Jan/Feb 2001, pp. 160-77; and C. Fred Bergsten, "America's Two-Front Economic Conflict," *Foreign Affairs*, Vol. 80, No. 2, March/April 2001, pp. 16-27.

7. Evidence of the positive effects of globalization is still in dispute. Lael Brainard, "Smoothing the Rough Edges of Globalization," lecture delivered to the University of Baltimore School of Law, November 18, 2002, suggests that the poverty gap between nations has grown, but that the living standards, life spans, and incomes have risen across the board. See also Anne O. Krueger, First Deputy Managing Director of the International Monetary Fund, who maintained that the poor are

actually getting wealthier at a rate faster than the rich; presentation delivered at the Eisenhower Conference, September 26, 2002, Washington, DC. Stephen J. Flanagan, Director of the Institute for National Strategic Studies, disputed Krueger's claims; presentation delivered at the same conference.

8. Consider, for example, that while globalization has brought greater prosperity to some parts of the world, it has also contributed to the rapid spread of the Asian economic flu. Even if this crisis has passed, a full recovery might still take considerable time. Sheldon W. Simon, *The Economic Crisis and ASEAN States' Security*, Carlisle, PA: Strategic Studies Institute, 1998. One should also remember that, despite a decade's worth of effort, a free market economy has still not taken hold in Russia, owing to an ineffective government, a well-entrenched organized crime syndicate, and growing regional fragmentation, among other problems. Tensions in the Middle East, where democracy has precious few footholds, have recently risen quite dramatically, threatening to erupt in a broader military and political crisis. While democracy has made rapid strides in Central and South America, economic change has actually exacerbated social inequalities. And corruption and narco-trafficking remain stubborn problems. In Africa, economic growth has been uneven and intrastate violence has been extremely bloody. *Strategic Assessment 1999: Priorities for a Turbulent World,* Washington, DC: Institute for National Strategic Studies, National Defense University, 1999, pp. xi-xiv, pp. 69-188; *New World Coming: American Security in the 21st Century: Supporting Research & Analysis,* Washington, DC: U.S. Commission on National Security/21st Century, September 15, 1999, pp. 59-116; and Jacquelyn K. Davis and Michael J. Sweeney, *Strategic Paradigms 2025: U.S. Security Planning for a New Era,* Washington, DC: Institute for Foreign Policy Analysis, 1999, pp. 33-174.

9. Richard Faulk and Andrew Strauss, "Toward Global Parliament," *Foreign Affairs*, Vol. 80, No. 1, Jan/Feb 2001, pp. 212-220.

10. The Kosovo campaign required the marshalling of considerable political and military resources from the entire NATO Alliance. If supported by a larger state or a network of transnational forces or if armed with weapons of mass destruction, a small state like Serbia could have presented much greater challenges, even for an alliance as large as NATO. Of course, such adversaries could also employ so-called asymmetric weapons or strategies, which might make the challenge even greater. See Kenneth F. McKenzie, Jr., *The Revenge of the Melians: Asymmetric Threats and the Next QDR*, Washington, DC: Institute for National Strategic Studies, 2000; and Steven Metz and Douglas Johnson, *Asymmetry and U.S. Military Strategy: Definition,*

Background, and Strategic Concepts, Carlisle, PA: Strategic Studies Institute, U.S. Army War College, 2001.

11. Samuel P. Huntington, *The Clash of Civilizations and the Remaking of World Order*, New York: Simon & Schuster, 1996; and Robert Kaplan, *The Coming Anarchy: Shattering the Dreams of the Post-Cold War World*, New York: Random House, 2000. Huntington is balanced by Richard E. Rubenstein, "Challenging Huntington," *Foreign Policy*, Vol. 96, 1994, pp. 113-128; *Strategic Assessment 1999*, p. xi; *New World Coming*, 1999; Davis and Sweeney, *Strategic Paradigms 2025*, 1999; Sam J. Tangredi, *All Possible Wars? Toward a Consensus View of the Future Security Environment, 2001-2025*, Washington, DC: National Defense University, 2000; and *Global Trends 2015: A Dialogue about the Future*, *http://www.cia.gov/cia/publications/globaltrends2015*.

12. Dr. Ray Kurzweil maintains that the decade from 2000-2010 will see as much change as the entire 20th century. Presentation entitled, "The Law of Accelerating Returns and its Impact on War & Peace," delivered at the 23rd Army Science Conference, December 4, 2002.

13. See, for example, *The U.S. National Military Strategy*, Pre-decisional Draft, October 16, 2002, pp. 3-5.

14. Collectively, international terrorists were responsible for 348 attacks during 2001, with the casualty total reaching an all-time high of 4,655, due to the attacks of September 11, 2001. U.S. Department of State, *Patterns of Global Terrorism 2001*, May 2002, p. xx, *http://www.state.gov/s/ct/rls/pgtrpt*. According to the FBI's Counter-terrorism and Counterintelligence Directorate, the United States also faces "significant challenges" from domestic terrorists. From 1980 to 2000, a total of 335 terrorist (or suspected terrorist) incidents occurred in the United States, 247 of which were attributed to domestic terrorists. Dale L. Watson, Executive Assistant Director, Counterterrorism and Counterintelligence, FBI, "The Terrorist Threat Confronting the United States," Testimony before the Senate Select Committee on Intelligence, February 6, 2002, pp. 2-5.

15. Today's terrorists also appear less constrained and more informed than those of the 1960s-1970s, having learned from their methods, and mistakes. While the number of deaths per terrorist incident has risen over time, one should not conclude from this trend that future terrorists will *only* attack in ways that result in mass casualties. Rod Probst, "New Terrorists, New Attack Means: Categorizing Terrorist Challenges for the Early 21st Century," *Journal of Homeland Security*, March 22, 2002.

16. *http://www.cdi.org/issues/nukef&f/database/nukearsenals. html*. See also *Global Trends 2015*.

17. Donald H. Rumsfeld, *et al.*, *The Report of the Commission to Assess the Ballistic Missile Threat to the United States*, Washington, DC, July 15, 1998, pp. 8-9; and Michael O'Hanlon, "Cruise Control: A Case for Missile Defense," *The National Interest*, No. 67, April 2002, *http://www.nationalinterest.org/issues/67/Ohanlon.html*.

18. As the congressional testimony of Carl W. Ford, Jr., Assistant Secretary of State for Intelligence and Research, indicated, biological weapons appeal to many states and will grow in importance because they "are relatively cheap, easy to disguise within commercial ventures, and potentially as devastating as nuclear weapons." Statement before the Senate Committee on Foreign Relations on the topic of "Reducing the Threat of Chemical and Biological Weapons," March 19, 2002, p. 3.

19. Press briefing by John S. Wolf, Assistant Secretary of State For Nonproliferation Issues, at the Foreign Press Center, Washington, DC, April 16, 2002. Despite the chemical and biological weapons conventions, concerns remain over clandestine programs and the absence of Middle Eastern and North-east Asian states as signatories. Jonathan B. Tucker and Kathleen M. Vogel, "Preventing the Proliferation of Chemical and Biological Weapon Materials and Know-How," *The Nonproliferation Review*, Vol. 7, No. 1, Spring 2000, pp. 88-96, esp. p. 95; Marie I. Chevier, "Strengthening the International Arms Control Regime," in *Biological Warfare: Modern Offense and Defense*, Raymond A. Zilinskas, ed., Boulder: Lynne Reinner, 2000, pp. 149-176.

20. Mohan Malik, *Dragon on Terrorism: Assessing China's Tactical Gains and Strategic Losses Post-September 11*, Carlisle, PA: U.S. Army War College, Strategic Studies Institute, 2002, p. 50. Amy Smithson and Leslie-Anne Levy, *Ataxia: The Chemical and Biological Terrorism Threat and the US Response*, Stimson Center Report No. 35, October 2000; and *Hype or Reality? The 'New Terrorism' and Mass Casualty Attacks*, ed., Brad Roberts, Alexandria, VA: 2000, caution that weaponizing chemical and biological materials is difficult. Yet, acquiring them is far from impossible. Felgenhauer, "Do the Terrorists Have Nukes?" *Wall Street Journal*, November 8, 2001, p. A-24. This is particularly true of radiological or "dirty" bombs. Paul Richter, "Studying 'Dirty' Bomb Scenario," *Los Angeles Times*, April 24, 2002. We should not forget that a number of Western arms suppliers are also responsible for current nonproliferation challenges. Hugh Williamson, "German Newspaper Lists Iraqi Arms Suppliers," *Financial Times*, December 17, 2002.

21. United States General Accounting Office, *MAD COW DISEASE: Improvements in the Animal Feed Ban and Other Regulatory Areas Would Strengthen U.S. Prevention Efforts*, Washington, DC: GAO, January 2002, pp. 3-4. In total, U.S. agriculture netted $215 billion in 1999. The U.S. Census Bureau 2001, p. 537.

22. Eric Lichtbau, "CIA Warns of Chinese Plans for Cyber-Attacks on U.S." *Los Angeles Times*, April 25, 2002.

23. The Government Accounting Office and the National Security Agency currently assess U.S. federal cyber defenses as inadequate. "GAO Reports on Information Security Audits," *Homeland Security Monitor*, April 19, 2002.

24. Author's translation. The German text is: "Der Krieg ist eine bloße Fortsetzung der Politik mit anderen Mitteln." *Vom Kriege Hinterlassenes Werk des Generals Carl von Clausewitz*, 19th Ed., ed. and intro. by Werner Hahlweg, Bonn: Ferd. Dümmlers Verlag, 1980, p. 210. Hereafter, *Vom Kriege*. For examples of the central place of politics in the nature of war, see Bernard Brodie, "A Guide to the Reading of On War," in Carl von Clausewitz, *On War*, ed. and trans. by Michael Howard and Peter Paret, Princeton: Princeton University Press, 1976, pp. 641-656; Eliot A. Cohen, *Citizens and Soldiers: The Dilemmas of Military Service*, Ithaca: Cornell University Press, 1985, pp. 22-24, which maintains that "politics pervades war and the preparation for it" and "Strategy: Causes, Conduct, and Termination of War," in *Security Studies for the 21st Century*, ed. by Richard H. Shultz, Jr., Roy Godson, George H. Quester, Washington, DC: Brassey's, 1997, pp. 364-366, which uses "politics" as the defining element in war; and Colin S. Gray, *Modern Strategy*, Oxford: Oxford University Press, 1999, who places it at the center of his definition and concept of strategy.

25. See Colin Powell, *My American Journey: An Autobiography*, New York: Random House, 1995; Wesley K. Clark, *Waging Modern War: Bosnia, Kosovo, and the Future of Combat*, New York: Public Affairs, 2001. Clausewitz's concepts concerning the nature of war and the primacy of politics are also stressed as part of the curricula at most of the U.S. military's command and staff colleges and war colleges.

26. See, for example, Colonel Joseph I. Greene, "Foreword" to Karl von Clausewitz, *On War*, trans., O. J. Matthijs Jolles, New York: Modern Library, 1943, p. xiii.

27. That view is still prevalent today; see Colonel James K. Greer, "Operational Art for the Objective Force," *Military Review*, September-October 2002, pp. 22-29, esp. p. 24.

28. See, for example, G.F. Freudenberg, "A Conversation with General Clausewitz," *Military Review*, Vol. 57, No. 10, October 1977, pp. 68-71.

29. Christopher Bassford, *Clausewitz in English: The Reception of Clausewitz in Britain and America, 1815-1945*, Oxford: Oxford University Press, 1994. Stuart Kinross, *Clausewitz and the American Military Tradition*, Ph.D. Dissertation, Kings College, 2002, Chapters 1 and 3. The classic example is Harry G. Summers, Jr., *On Strategy: A Critical Analysis of the Vietnam War*, Novato, CA: Presidio, 1995.

30. John Keegan, *A History of Warfare*, New York: Alfred A. Knopf, 1994. See also Martin van Creveld, *The Transformation of War*, New York: Free Press, 1991, esp. pp. 33-62.

31. Keegan, *Warfare*, p. 24.

32. *Ibid.*, p. 46.

33. Much of the literature dealing with the nature of war actually fails to differentiate between war and the weapons used to wage it. William E. Odom, *America's Military Revolution: Strategy and Structure after the Cold War,* Washington, DC: American University, 1993, purports to discuss the changing nature of war, but really only addresses changes in weaponry; Martin van Creveld, "Through a Glass Darkly: Some Reflections on the Future of War," *Naval War College Review*, Vol. LIII, No. 4, Autumn 2000, pp. 25-44, in effect, only includes changing forms of war when discussing changes in the nature of war; and the Cantigny Conference Series, *The Changing Nature of Conflict*, Chicago: Robert R. McCormick Tribune Foundation, 1995, p. 32, actually only discusses changes in war's root causes.

34. Van Creveld, *Transformation of War*, pp. 124-126; and "The Transformation of War Revisited," *Small Wars and Insurgencies,* Vol. 13, No. 2, Summer 2002, pp. 3-15, esp. pp. 12-13.

35. Russell Weigley, "The Political and Strategic Dimensions of Military Effectiveness," in *Military Effectiveness*, ed., Williamson Murray and Allan R. Millett, Boston: Allen and Unwin, 1988, Vol. 3, *The Second World War*, p. 341.

36. Clausewitz, *Vom Kriege*, Book I, Chap. 1, pp. 211-12.

37. Peter Paret, *Clausewitz and the State: The Man, His Theories, and His Times*, Princeton: Princeton University Press, 1985, p. 154, noted that Clausewitz used the same objective-subjective construct in an earlier (1804) essay entitled "Strategie und Taktik," Strategy and

Tactics. This construct was not uncommon in Clausewitz's day, particularly in philosophical discourse. It was used in the works of Immanuel Kant, for example, from whom Clausewitz borrowed several analytical tools; for example, compare *Vom Kriege*, Book I, Chapter 3, "Military Genius," to Kant's description of genius in the *Critique of Judgment*, Sections 46-50. Under Kant's system, *objective* laws were those recognized as valid for the will of every rational being. *Subjective* laws were those regarded as valid only for an individual; see Book I, Chapter I, Section 1 and the Table of Categories in the *Critique of Pure Practical Reason*.

38. *Vom Kriege*, Book I, Chap. 1, p. 213.

39. For a correct interpretation of the trinity, see Christopher Bassford and Edward J. Villacres, "Reclaiming the Clausewitzian Trinity," *http://www.clausewitz.com/CWZHOME/Keegan/KEEGWHOL.htm.*

40. Author's translation: *Vom Kriege*, Book I, Chap. 1, p. 213. Readers may also find the term "wunderlich" translated as "remarkable" as it is in the first edition of Howard and Paret's translation of *On War* (1976) or as "paradoxical" as it is in the second edition (1989).

41. *Ibid.*, pp. 212-213.

42. *Ibid.*, Book VIII, Chap. 3B, pp. 962, 964-965.

43. On Clausewitz's division of *Politik* into objective and subjective factors, see E. Kessel, "Zur Genesis der modernen Kriegslehren" [On the Genesis of Modern Military Theories], *Wehrwissenschaftliche Rundschau*, Vol. 3, No. 9, July 1953, p. 405-423, esp. pp. 410-417.

44. *Vom Kriege*, Book VIII, Chap. 3B, pp. 961-962.

45. *Ibid.*, p. 974. The last three books of *On War* (Defense, Attack, and War Plans) reflect Clausewitz's increasingly historicist perspective, that is, that historical eras must be understood on their own terms. There is, therefore, no single, correct type of war. Instead, the kind of war that occurs in a particular era—such as a limited war in the 18th century—is valid for that era.

46. *Ibid.*

47. Douglas S. Benson, *The Tartar War*, Chicago: Maverick Publishing, 1981.

48. "Al-Qaeda (the Base)," *http://www.ict.org.il/inter_ter/orgdet. cfm*. George J. Tenet, Director, CIA, "Worldwide Threat—Converging Dangers in a Post 9/11 World," Testimony before the Senate Armed Services Committee, March 19, 2002, pp. 2-3.

49. Van Creveld, *Transformation of War*, pp. 192-233.

50. "Anticipatory Defense in the War on Terror: Interview with Condolezza Rice," *New Perspectives Quarterly*, Vol. 19, No. 3, Fall 2002, pp. 5-8; Tom Barnet, "Where—Not When—Preemption Makes Sense," *Transformation Trends*, November 18, 2002; The White House, *National Strategy to Combat Weapons of Mass Destruction*, Washington, DC: December 2002, p. 3.

51. Brian Michael Jenkins, *Countering al Qaeda: An Appreciation of the Situation and Suggestions for Strategy*, Santa Monica, CA: RAND, 2002, p. 7.

52. Although, by their nature, cells tend to operate independently, the capability does exist for a political leader such as Osama bin Laden to communicate with those cells.

53. Ed Blanche, "Al-Qaeda Recruitment," *Jane's Intelligence Review*, Vol. 14, January 2002, pp. 27-28; Paul J. Smith, "Transnational Terrorism and the al Qaeda Model: Confronting New Realities," *Parameters*, Vol. XXXII, No. 2, Summer 2002, pp. 33-46.

54. Also, new activities suggest at least indirect Al Qaeda involvement: threats against U.S. embassies in Southeast Asia; the October 2 bombing in an open-air market in Zamboanga, Philippines; the October 6 explosion aboard the French supertanker *Limburg* in a Yemeni port; two shooting incidents involving U.S. Marines off the coast of Kuwait and the October 12 car bombing outside a nightclub in Bali which killed nearly 200 people, many of them Westerners. "String of Violence Highlights Core Problems in Battle Against Al Qaeda," *http://www.stratfor.com/corp*.

55. Rohan Gunaratna, *Inside Al Qaeda: Global Network of Terror*, New York: Columbia, 2002, pp. 55, 227.

56. Reportedly, Osama became a popular name for new babies. Jenkins, *Countering Al Qaeda*, p. 7. Yet, the spontaneous uprisings that bin Laden apparently hoped for have not materialized.

57. Gunaratna, *Inside Al Qaeda*, p. 230.

58. Smith, "Transnational Terrorism," p. 45.

59. "World War IV," an address delivered at the National War College by James Woolsey, November 16, 2002. Woolsey considers the Cold War to have been World War III.

60. "Searching for Answers, US Intelligence After September 11: A Conversation with [Senator] Bob Graham," *Harvard International Review*, Vol. XXIV, No. 3, Fall 2002, pp. 40-43.

61. The Director of the Defense Intelligence Agency emphasized that the "strategic attack" of September 11, 2001, was carried out "not by the military forces of a rival state, but by a shadowy, global network of extremists, who struck unprotected targets, using methods we did not anticipate." Vice Admiral Thomas R. Wilson, "Global Threats and Challenges," Statement for the Record, U.S. Senate Armed Services Committee, March 19, 2002, p. 2.

62. Kip P. Nygren, "Emerging Technologies and Exponential Change: Implications for Army Transformation," *Parameters*, Vol. XXXII, No. 2, Summer 2002, pp. 86-99.

63. Steven Biddle, *Afghanistan and the Future of Warfare: Implications for the Army and Defense Policy*, Carlisle, PA: U.S. Army War College, Strategic Studies Institute, 2002.

64. Antulio J. Echevarria II, "Clausewitz's Center of Gravity: It's *Not* What We Thought!" *Naval War College Review*, Vol. LVI, No. 1, Winter 2003, pp. 71-79.

65. Gunaratna, *Inside Al Qaeda*, pp. 76-77.

66. The Department of Health and Human Services is now considering using Dr. Donald Ainslie Henderson's "ring" strategy to combat any future outbreaks of contagious diseases. His strategy is credited with having eradicated smallpox. J. D. Reed, "Virus Vanquisher," *Smithsonian Magazine*, February 2002. See also Charles V. Lanza, William P. Johnson, and Niel H. Batista, "Smallpox: A Global Problem with Local Solutions, Parts I-III," *Homeland Defense Journal*, April 9, 2002.

67. ANSER Institute for Homeland Security, "Dark Winter" briefing, which describes an exercise that took place at Andrews Air Force Base, June 22-23, 2001; its casualty estimates were validated by an outside source: Tara O'Toole, Michael Mair, and Thomas V. Ingelsby, "Shining Light on 'Dark Winter'," *Confronting Biological Weapons*, electronically published by Clinical Infectious Diseases, February 19, 2002.

68. This is not to say that linear methods are never appropriate. On the contrary, they will prove useful much of the time and may often complement nonlinear strategies.

69. Discussions concerning defense and attack appear numerous places throughout *Vom Kriege*, but receive special attention in Book VI, Chapters 1-5; Book I, Chapter 1; Book VII, Chaps. 1-2; and Book VIII, Chap. 8.

70. *Ibid.*, Book VII, Chap. 2; and Book VI, Chap. 1.